FORMS OF GOVERNMENT: NEED TO KNOW

OLIGARCHY

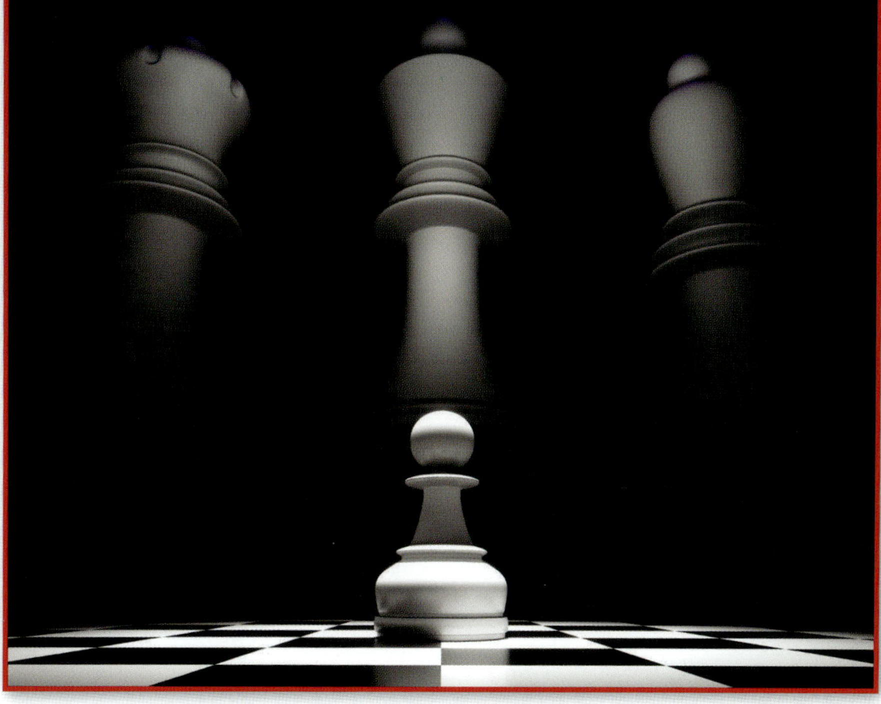

by D. R. Faust

Consultant: Caitlin Krieck, Social Studies Teacher and Instructional Coach, The Lab School of Washington

SilverTip Books, an imprint of Bearport Publishing by FlutterBee

Credits
Cover and title page, © EvilWata/iStock; 3, © PeskyMonkey/Shutterstock; 5, © monkeybusinessimages/iStock; 7–8, © Public Domain/Wikimedia Commons; 9, © DEA/G. DAGLI ORTI/Getty Images; 11, © MeijiShowa/Alamy Stock Photo; 13, © Nastasic/Getty Images; 15, © SPCOLLECTION/Alamy Stock Photo; 17, © Les Archives Digitales/Alamy Stock Photo; 19, © imageBROKER.com/Alamy Stock Photo; 20, © gracethang2/Shutterstock; 21, © World History Archive/Alamy Stock Photo; 22–23, © Xinhua/Alamy Stock Photo; 25, © Handout/Getty Images; 27, © EBRAHIM HAMID/Getty Images.

Bearport Publishing Company Product Development Team
Kayla Eggert, Theresa Emminizer, Kim Jones, Allison Juda, Cole Nelson, Naomi Reich, Steve Scheluchin, Tiana Tran

Statement on Usage of Generative Artificial Intelligence
Bearport Publishing remains committed to publishing high-quality nonfiction books. Therefore, we restrict the use of generative AI to ensure accuracy of all text and visual components pertaining to a book's subject. See BearportPublishing.com for details.

Library of Congress Cataloging-in-Publication Data is available at www.loc.gov or upon request from the publisher.

ISBN: 979-8-89577-638-4 (hardcover)
ISBN: 979-8-89577-792-3 (paperback)
ISBN: 979-8-89577-726-8 (ebook)

Copyright © 2026 Bearport Publishing Company. All rights reserved. No part of this publication may be reproduced in whole or in part, stored in any retrieval system, or transmitted in any form or by any means, electronic, mechanical, photocopying, recording, or otherwise, without written permission from the publisher. Bearport Publishing is a division of FlutterBee Education Group.

For more information, write to Bearport Publishing, 3500 American Blvd W, Suite 150, Bloomington, MN 55431. Printed in the United States of America.

Contents

The Few in Charge

Imagine if a small group of your classmates got to make all the school rules. Or if only a few of your teammates decided on every play during a soccer game. Sometimes, this happens in governments. A few powerful people run everything. This is called an oligarchy (AH-li-*gar*-key).

Oligarchies have been around for a long time. The first person to talk about them was Aristotle. He wrote about this kind of government in the fourth century BCE.

Ruling Classes

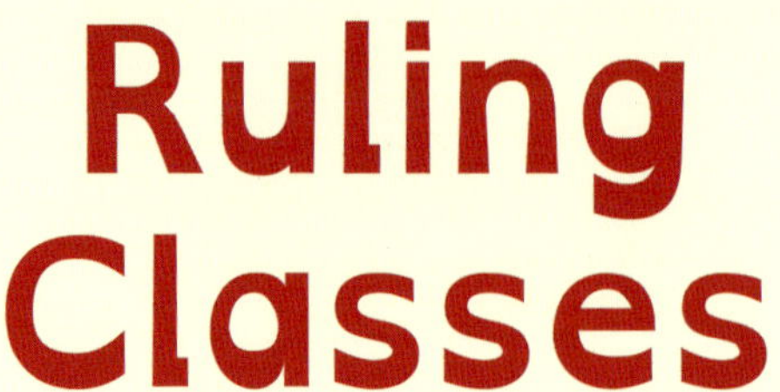

The small group in charge of an oligarchy is called the ruling class. This group runs everything. Only people from the ruling class can make laws. All of the top government leaders are part of this group. And they are chosen by others from this class.

Many forms of government have powerful groups of people. But the ruling class gets complete control in an oligarchy.

Most people in a place with an oligarchy are not in this ruling class. They have very little power over what happens. These people cannot choose their leaders. They often do not get a say in which laws are made. But they must still follow these laws.

The ruling class may make laws that make life harder for many people. They can set high **taxes**. They may take away basic **rights**.

The ruling class might collect taxes.

Many Ways to Rule

Members of a ruling class share something in common. This sets them apart from everybody else. But it is not always the same thing. The reason the ruling class has power can be different from government to government.

Often, members of the ruling class pass their power to a family member. A child may take the place of their parent. This keeps the same group in charge as time goes on.

Japan was an oligarchy from 1192 to 1867.

The Best and the Rest

The first oligarchies formed thousands of years ago. In ancient Greece, they thought some people were naturally better leaders. They said this group was smarter. The Greeks thought they could make better laws. They called them the **aristocracy** (ar-i-STAH-kruh-see). This also became the name of the form of government.

The word *oligarchy* comes from ancient Greek. It means rule by a few. The **city-state** of Sparta in Greece had an oligarchy.

The Greek aristocracy was made up of a few powerful families.

Rule by the Rich

Many oligarchies have the richest people in charge. These types of governments are called **plutocracies**. The rich ruling class often uses their power to make more money. They may make laws to keep themselves rich and in charge. This also keeps everyone else poor and powerless.

Italy was made of many city-states from 1300 to 1600. One was Venice. Only rich business owners could make laws in Venice.

Ancient Roman lawmakers were often well-off business owners.

All in the Family

Some oligarchies stay in the family. The ruling class is made up of a small group of families. Government jobs are held by members of this group. Parents pass power down to their children. This keeps the ruling class the same.

> Power in a **monarchy** is often passed along in a family. However, this form of government has one person in charge. An oligarchy has a group.

Race and Oligarchies

Some oligarchies are run by members of the same social category. The ruling class may share the same **ethnicity**. They may be members of the same race. These oligarchies often happen when an outside force takes over. The ruling class is from this other group.

The Mongols attacked China in the thirteenth century. They became the new ruling class. This group held power for more than 100 years.

Rulers from Mongolia took over China in the 1200s.

South Africa had an oligarchy based on race starting in 1948. The white ruling class took away the rights of non-white people. They set up laws that limited almost everything Black South Africans could do. This system was called **apartheid** (uhh-PARR-tide). It lasted until 1994.

Nelson Mandela was a Black South African. He led fighting against apartheid. When it ended, the government changed to a **democracy**. Mandela was named the first Black president of South Africa.

Laws limited where Black South Africans could go.

Might Makes Right

There are also some military oligarchies. These places are under the control of the armed forces. The top leaders in the government are from the army. These types of governments often use force to keep control.

The military controls the government in Myanmar. The prime minister is a top general. Many of the lawmakers are chosen by the military.

From On High

Religious leaders form the ruling class in some places. This is called a **theocracy**. Leaders in this form of government make laws that line up with their religious beliefs. They may even outlaw other religions.

These governments can form under different religions. There are Buddhist, Islamic, and Catholic theocracies. The laws are different in each.

Ali Khamenei leads Iran's Islamic theocracy.

A Mixed Bag

Like all forms of government, the role of oligarchies has shifted over time. Some places have turned away from oligarchies. Others have put new ones in place. But it is clear that both government leaders and the world are changing. And they will continue to do so in the future.

As oligarchies change, they may include pieces from different forms of government. In fact, there are few governments around the world that do not have a blend of forms.

Sudan was a democracy until 2021. It is now run by a military oligarchy.

Forms of Oligarchy

There are many forms of oligarchies. Let's look at a few.

FORM OF OLIGARCHY	RULING CLASS	EXAMPLES
Aristocracy	Those considered the best	Ancient Greece
Military oligarchy	Members of the military	Myanmar
Plutocracy	The wealthy	Venice from about 1300 to 1600
Racial oligarchy	Members of a race or ethnicity	Apartheid South Africa
Theocracy	Religious leaders	Iran

SilverTips for SUCCESS

★ SilverTips for REVIEW

Review what you've learned. Use the text to help you.

Define key terms

apartheid
aristocracy
plutocracy
ruling class
theocracy

Check for understanding

What is the name given to the group in charge of an oligarchy?

Give two examples of members that can make up a ruling class.

Explain the difference between an aristocracy and a plutocracy.

Think deeper

How might your life be different if the style of government in your city, state, or nation changed?

★ SilverTips for TAKING TESTS

- **Make a study plan.** Ask your teacher what the test is going to cover. Then, set aside time to study a little bit every day.
- **Read all the questions carefully.** Be sure you know what is being asked.
- **Skip any questions** you don't know how to answer right away. Mark them and come back later if you have time.

Glossary

apartheid a former system in South Africa where political and economic rights were based on race

aristocracy an upper class that is more powerful than the rest of society

city-state a state that has its own government and is made up of a city and the surrounding area

democracy a form of government in which the people have the power to make decisions

ethnicity relating to a group of people who have the same customs, religion, or homeland

monarchy a form government with a single royal leader

plutocracies governments that are run by the richest people

rights the basic things people have a claim to

taxes money paid by the people to the government

theocracy a form of government shaped by religion

Read More

Davis, Jane R. *Ten Terrible Kings and Queens (History's Very Worst).* Buffalo, NY: Gareth Stevens Publishing, 2026.

Gitlin, Marty. *Ancient Rulers Who Wrecked the World (Ancient Worlds).* Ann Arbor, MI: 45th Parallel Press, 2025.

Scott, David. *Government Around the World (Social Studies: Informational Text).* Huntington Beach, CA: Teacher Created Materials, Inc., 2023.

Learn More Online

1. Go to **FactSurfer.com** or scan the QR code below.
2. Enter "**Oligarchy**" into the search box.
3. Click on the cover of this book to see a list of websites.

Index

About the Author

D. R. Faust is a freelance writer of fiction and nonfiction. They live in Queens, NY.